A SOLUTION TO AFFORDABLE HOUSING

James W. Lewis

A SOLUTION TO AFFORDABLE HOUSING

© 2023, James W. Lewis.

Print ISBN: 979-8-35092-971-3

eBook ISBN: 979-8-35092-972-0

CONTENTS

INTRODUCTION

I N 333 B.C., ALEXANDER THE GREAT FACED AND solved the Gordian Knot challenge. At that time, untying that famous knot was thought to be an insurmountable problem, but Alexander's creative and decisive actions convinced his world that there was a simple solution.

The many problems preventing all citizens from obtaining affordable housing are today's Gordian Knot challenge. These problems are entangled so tightly and are metastasizing so rapidly that solutions now being offered to make progress in specific problem areas often have negative impacts in other problem areas. Political differences and the blame game are the common result, and a rapidly growing segment of our population experiences the crippling effects of unaffordable and inadequate housing.

Affordable housing is defined as housing that does not take more than 30 percent of an owner's pre-tax income to pay the sum of mortgage payments, property taxes, and insurance or more than 30 percent of a renter's pre-tax income to pay rent.

This book is burdened by being only a snapshot in time in a rapidly changing and unprecedented economic environment. To put the size of today's affordable housing problem in perspective, consider that less than half (about 40 percent) of new and existing homes sold in Q2, 2023 were affordable to families earning the median income of $96,300 according to the National Association of Home Builders (NAHB). From June 2020 to June 2023, the median existing home price has appreciated by 39.3 percent while the 30-year fixed mortgage rate has increased by 127 percent over the same period. Based on analyzing both prices and rates together, the 3-year average mortgage cost has increased by 115.7 percent. As 30-year mortgage rates moved beyond 7 percent in 2023 (the highest rate since 2001), monthly mortgage payments exceeded $2,300. At the same time single-family monthly rental rates also reached $2,300. The Mortgage Bankers Association (MBA) expects that after a twenty-year record purchase origination total of $4.57 trillion in 2021, mortgage volume fell to $2.75 trillion in 2022. MBA expects a further decline to $1.41 trillion in 2023 and a rise to 1.67 trillion in 2024. The National Association of Realtors (NAR) economist Lawrence Yun has suggested that mortgage rates could soon reach 8.5 percent and he expects no home-price appreciation in 2023. He cites the fact that 99 percent of mortgage debt at the end of 2022 was locked in at 5 percent or less as another deterrent to home sales. This chaos is certainly confusing to economists and homebuyers alike, but it cannot be an excuse for accepting anything other than a long-term solution to the problem of affordable housing.

Many consider affordable housing to be a basic human right and will expect the solution offered here to deliver results in good times and hard times, no matter how those definitions play out in the future.

The eighteenth-century philosopher Arthur Schopenhauer said, "All truths pass through three stages. First, it is ridiculed. Second, it is violently opposed. Third it is accepted as being self-evident."

With that idea in mind, let's examine the many facets of this seemingly unsolvable problem followed by providing a solution informed by the past and by the rapidly changing dynamics of money and markets today. Success can be measured by how easy and scalable adoption of the solution is in changing the course of future events. No solution can ever reverse the negative events of the past, but common sense and time can heal the wounds. Be advised that there is no treasure map here, and the solution offered will be a disappointment to readers who approach the problem with only the question of "How can we make money from this?"

SECTION 1:

AFFORDABLE HOUSING PROBLEMS

Some Real,
Some Misunderstood

CHAPTER 1

HOUSING PRICES OUTPACING WAGE GAINS

N OT ONLY ARE HOUSING PRICES OUTPACING WAGE gains, but past disparities have also resulted in a very difficult starting point to launch any solution to the lack of affordable housing. In their October 2021 report, *The State of the State's Housing Market*, the Kem C. Gardner Policy Institute at the University of Utah reported that by the end of 2020, the median home price had reached $380,000—pricing out 48.5 percent of Utah households. In 2019, 63 percent of renter households were priced out of the median home price rental, and that increased to 73 percent in 2020. That may sound a bit alarming but consider that the Utah median home price had risen to $564,000 in 2022 and the 3.1 percent mortgage rate had increased to 5.5 percent by the summer of 2022, raising the qualifying annual income at the 30 percent affordability standard from around $51,000 to over $102,000 for an 80 percent LTV thirty-year fixed rate mortgage. In 2023 the median home price fell to $526,000, but mortgage rates at 7 percent raised the qualifying annual income to over $112,000. In 2023, ZipRecruiter reported the average annual salary in Utah to be $48,243 with top earners (ninetieth percentile) making $74,374. Utah renter households saw a 17.2 percent increase in rents in 2021. By July 2022, the national median asking rent for SFR homes exceeded $2,000 per month, so housing affordability continues to be elusive for renters.

Looking at the nation as a whole and using the 30 percent of household income standard, only six U.S. states in late 2021/early 2022 had median incomes high enough to afford the median monthly mortgage payment.

The Kem C. Gardner Policy Institute has referred to the current time as the "Platinum Age" for Utah's real estate industry and other winners in the housing surge. The 70 percent of Utah households priced out of home ownership or Single-Family Rental (SFR) tenancy might not share the enthusiasm for this platinum age. Many of these households seem to be joining the ranks of those with growing resistance to unfettered growth. A 2021 Envision Utah survey of 800 representative Utah adults showed that 46 percent favor management or curbs on growth, up from 28 percent in 2015. Compared to the 59 percent who supported it in 2014, only 38 percent stated that growth should be encouraged. Politically, Utah identifies as a very conservative, heavily Republican state, but surprisingly, baby boomers and those with relatively high incomes were more likely to feel that growth is increasingly negative and should be managed or limited. This group is known for large families and is very concerned that their kids and grandkids might not be able to live near them. Many of those swelling Utah's in-migration numbers are coming from California. According to Envision Utah, increasing resistance to growth could lead to policies and practices, either statewide or in local communities, similar to California's recent experience. They have also stated that California's history shows that attempts to limit growth by reducing new housing drives up the cost of housing and makes housing less affordable, less attainable, and less equitable.

Despite higher wages being earned by many members of the growing in-migration being recruited from California and other high-tech areas, many of these incoming households are forced to be renters by necessity. Utah was the fastest-growing state in the nation from 2010 to 2020 at 18.4 percent, and net in-migration accounted for 35 percent of that growth, but in 2021, the in-migration component nearly doubled. Even these fortunate new residents face obstacles like student debt, lack of down payment, or credit scores needed to get a warm welcome from lenders.

CHAPTER 2

RISING HOUSING INEQUALITY

U TAH'S ESTIMATED 700,000 EXISTING HOMEOWNERS saw their combined home equity increase by about $82 billion in 2021. The average homeowner's net worth increased by about $113,000 in 2021. According to the 2019 Survey of Consumer Finances, the median Utah homeowner had a net worth of $255,000 in 2019, while the median Utah renter's net worth was only $6,300, The Survey of Consumers Finances is conducted every three years by the Board of Governors of the Federal Reserve System. The 2022 survey is expected in late 2023 and the large home price increases since 2019 should only widen this homeowner/renter net-worth gap.

This classic haves versus have-not's situation often turns homeowners and renters into two enemy camps. When average homeowners can earn more than their earned wages from equity gains in their homes and those not able to qualify for homeownership find the goal of becoming residential property owners increasingly out of reach, it becomes a common occurrence for homeowners to protest any growth near their homes that they perceive as a threat to their accumulated home equity. Recently, many homeowners are choosing to join the ranks of small landlords (those who own between one and ten residential rental properties) by tapping into their home equity.

At the same time, the growing number of single-family rental homes (SFR) and built for rental homes (BFR) owned by large investment companies join small investors in competing with first-time homebuyers for the limited supply of homes. These investors in residential property they do not intend to occupy often have significant advantages in terms of resources and expertise. They engage in competition that contributes to rising home prices, as any homebuyer caught up in a multiple-offer situation has seen. Investors in residential property can compensate for paying higher home prices and carrying costs by becoming landlords who raise rents for their tenants based on the theory of "whatever the market will bear." As renters trying to become homeowners pay those higher rents, their financial ability to compete for future home ownership opportunities gradually weakens.

Most of the renters in Utah and nationally are not on the cusp of home ownership, rather they are largely renters by necessity who pay lower rents for older, smaller residences in less-desirable locations. Average rents continue to see unprecedented double-digit hikes year over year. The nonprofit Utah Foundation recently found that since 2019, rents have risen by as much as 50 percent in some pockets along the Wasatch Front, despite a boom in apartment construction. The most common new apartment units being built in the Salt Lake City area are two-bedroom units, with far fewer three-bedroom, one-bedroom, and studio floor plans. Lower-income renters, particularly those with children, must often accept fewer bedrooms, bathrooms, garage space, and yard area than is needed for their families in order to be able to afford rent payments. This group typically has a less secure income and faces greater risk of eviction. Rapidly rising rents and the end of government COVID-19 relief support are causing increasing numbers of renters to relocate to less-desirable rentals or even to drop into homelessness or reliance on subsidized housing.

Forty years ago, about 8 percent of young adults lived with their parents. In 2022, that number was 17 percent. During the pandemic, many younger people ceased renting and went back to live with their parents.

Operating the bank of Mom and Dad imposes significant financial burdens on older homeowners. Funding provided by borrowing against home equity to provide down-payment assistance for their children and grandchildren compounds the growing need to provide in-home health care for family members. According to the NAR, between 21 and 23 percent of first-time buyers are going directly from living with family to their own home without an extended stop in rental housing versus 12 to 15 percent between 1989 and 1995. Today there are 53 million family caregivers in the U.S. who provide an estimated $470 billion worth of free care. Nineteen percent of unpaid family caregivers are sixty-five and older, and 7 percent are over the age of seventy-five. Simple downsizing is less practical and more difficult in those situations, due to the home size needed to fulfill those family obligations. Borrowing for these needs reduces homeowner equity, and older homeowners find that affordable, smaller residential purchases or rentals are becoming harder to find in desired locations. The median annual cost of in-home health care was recently estimated to be $54,912, up 18.5 percent since 2016. Combined with the rapidly rising cost of family housing carrying costs and education assistance, these financial burdens are a significant problem for older, long-term homeowners.

Well-paid young homeowners being recruited by Utah's impressive list of tech-related businesses often meet the requirements for homeownership but prefer to rent in their first years of residence. As many as a third of these new residents opt out of home ownership for reasons that include:

- They want more flexibility to relocate. This often translates to not being sure that the offer of employment they receive will work out. Layoffs in Silicon Slopes tech employment in late 2022 and early 2023 validate this concern.

- They do not want to carry so much debt. This is often code for concerns about a poor or limited credit history, outstanding debt, or fear of rising interest rates.

- They do not want the responsibility of maintaining a home.

- They want to invest in something else or wish to avoid being a dual-income family.

As this group of renters-by-choice grows and prospers and their young children age, Utah's stock of largely smaller-floor plan, multifamily housing will not meet their family needs and they might choose to join the ranks of Utah's out-migration. This is another problem informed by California's recent history.

CHAPTER 3

BUILDERS AND DEVELOPERS

BUILDERS AND DEVELOPERS WHO WERE ONCE SEEN by most Utah citizens as a positive force who could build the state out of the affordable-housing problem are now often being unfairly blamed for rising prices and lack of inventory. Builders and developers in Utah and nationwide face a series of complicated problems of their own which must be solved if they are to survive as viable, profitable businesses.

According to a recent study from the National Association of Home Builders the U.S. has a 5.5 million home-housing deficit that will take years to erase. Based on the 2022 housing report from the NAR, that estimate has been raised to 6.5 million single-family homes short of population and household formation growth. MetLife estimates that 11 million new households will be formed in the U.S. over the next decade. MetLife also estimates that 4.5-million apartment units or single-family homes will be demolished over the next decade (primarily homes built before 1950), so there will be a demand for a minimum of 15.6 million new housing units in the next ten years. Considering the current housing deficit and household formation forecasts, estimates as high as 2.3 million new homes will be needed each year over the next ten years. That will be the challenge for the builders and developers of residential construction.

Standing in the way of meeting that challenge, Starwood Advisors estimated in November of 2021 that new home sales would likely fall below 800,000 units for the year and likely wouldn't accelerate much in the near term, based in part on the increasingly cumbersome entitlement processes in municipalities of all sizes. In 2022, 912,000 single-family homes were built. Going forward, would-be homeowners will be seriously constrained by soaring home prices, rising interest rates, and an estimated construction labor shortage of 1.5 million workers. Boomer construction labor is aging out of the workforce and being replaced by less-qualified younger generations, particularly in the skilled trades, who are demanding higher wages. According to an August 2022 survey by the Associated General Contractors of America and Autodesk, a staggering 93 percent of contractors have positions to fill, and 91 percent are having a hard time finding workers at all levels. Contractors believe that the root causes of remaining supply chain issues are driven by the shortage of qualified labor. Added to those problems, builders and developers are seeing a record-level shortage of developed lots. Construction items such as copper, lumber, steel, and cement saw extreme volatility and hyperinflation in 2021 that continued in 2022. For example, lumber prices surged 32 percent and the price of copper spiked by just over 50 percent in 2021. Overall, 2021 building material prices increased by more than 20 percent. Supply chain problems have contributed to the cost and delays in obtaining building materials produced in foreign locations. Recent COVID-19 pandemic problems and shipping cost volatility have improved but combined with a national shortage of truck drivers and continuing fuel price volatility, the critical need for re-examination of globalization and the fragile links in the supply chain are now in the spotlight. A new book by MIT professor Yossi Sheffi, entitled *The Magic Conveyor Belt: Supply Chains, A.I., and the Future of Work,* provides valuable insight into this problem.

There are an estimated 405,000 homebuilder businesses in the U.S. as of 2022. Of the 140,000 members of the NAHB 38,000 are builder members. Of those, 62 percent of builder members build single-family homes,

21 percent are residential remodelers, 6 percent are commercial builders, 4 percent are multifamily builders, and 4 percent are land developers. These NAHB members and the 265,000 builder businesses who are not members of the NAHB are often accused of being a part of the problem and of earning profits way beyond those needed to remain viable. Homebuilders face many problems, but with a few exceptions, are not the problem in affordable housing, rather they are an essential part of the solution, and that solution must help them to deal with the problems they face every day.

CHAPTER 4

BUSINESS OWNERS— VICTIMIZED AND IGNORED

EMPLOYERS FROM THE LARGEST TO THE SMALLEST have a unique problem regarding the affordable-housing crisis. They have always provided their employees with what they considered to be the answer to adequate housing: a paycheck. Many also provided pensions, good working conditions, and insurance benefits. In return, they expected company loyalty and hard work. Most employers did not appreciate union activity or worker complaints that paychecks were not adequate. For most companies, employee housing was a rare exception only justified by a company problem such as a mining project in a remote location. Some companies made a choice to profit from exploiting their own workforce—the company store in the coal-mining heyday. In the 1950s and 1960s, the thought that employers should even concern themselves with providing adequate housing for their employees was very rare. Company towns were just a faded memory and housing was not that expensive. If an employee had a steady paycheck, that employee could find or build a home with the help of a realtor and a mortgage lender.

As time went by and businesses grew, employers were forced by their investors to focus on maximizing short-term profits. Wall Street recognized that investors loved companies that produced ever-increasing quarterly profits. Business owners hired an army of executives and managers and rewarded them for minimizing wage costs in order to enhance profits. The goal shifted from making employees happy to making investors happy. An example of recent news that shows how far that trend has progressed is the Abbott baby formula uproar. Abbott's profit soared by 94 percent between 2019 and 2021, but after Abbott became aware of the tainted formula problem, it increased dividends to shareholders by more than 25 percent and announced a stock-buyback program worth $5 billion instead of making needed production investments. In the past, few companies understood or believed that there was long-term profit potential in making quality housing available and affordable to their employees. Fast forward to today and the growing realization that the wages needed to purchase the median-priced home are far higher than the wages being paid. Workers whose paycheck does not provide adequate housing and the other necessities of life are motivated to consider resignation and relocation if their demands for higher pay are not met. The dynamic of this conflict is the same whether the employee is a Starbucks barista or a recent MIT graduate interviewing for a starting position with a future.

Today the tech industry is a good example of the need for huge catch-up projects aimed at alleviating affordable housing problems for highly paid employees. Meta, the parent company of Facebook, is a good example with its $1 billion Willow Village project. Located near Meta's headquarters in Menlo Park, the project is planned to cover 1.6 million square feet at the current site of an industrial warehouse complex and will include a supermarket, a pharmacy, cafes, a 193-room hotel, and a town square. Surrounding the site will be 1.25 million square feet of new Meta office space and 1729 apartments. After the Menlo Park media stated that Meta's original design, which featured more office space and less housing, fit the definition of a company town of a century ago—a settlement where all stores and housing are owned by one company that also serves as the main employer—they continued their history lesson by saying that those mid-century company towns became a symbol of the overreach of American capitalism. They added that many so-called utopian settlements were exploitative and controlling, with residents' lives at the mercy of the corporation. This very dramatic media condemnation of historic company towns ended with statements claiming that after decreases in popularity and the collapse of the companies that built them, many ended up all but ghost towns.

Based on the charge that Meta was just another exploitive company looking to provide company housing for its employees, Menlo Park pushed back to insist Willow Village be public with more affordable and senior housing. Reworked plans estimate that 320 of the 1729 apartments will now be affordable. In the pursuit of Menlo Park government and neighboring resident approvals, Signature Development Group, the Oakland developers leading the project for Facebook, have changed the project from a Meta employee benefit to a vanilla, mixed-use development. The result is very little affordable housing for Meta employees at a gigantic cost to their employer. In December of 2022, the Menlo Park City Council unanimously approved Meta's new Willow Village development first proposed in 2020. At the same time, Meta Platforms announced it was eliminating 2,564 jobs in five of its Northern California facilities, including at its headquarters in Menlo Park. An outbreak of short-term thinking in Silicon Valley resulted in 8,000 layoffs in the fourth quarter of 2022 and 9,000 layoffs were expected in the first quarter of 2023. Those layoffs include many tech giants in addition to Meta—Amazon, Microsoft, Google, Cisco, Salesforce, Lyft, Oracle, Roku, DoorDash, PayPal, and GoFundMe. Clearly, a new battle is taking shape. Employers who follow the time-honored practice of laying off employees at any sign of a downturn will be up against a growing number of employers who believe in labor hoarding.

After a May 2019 Bloomberg article entitled "An RV Camp Sprang Up Outside Google's Headquarters, Now Mountain View wants to Ban It," Google has come up with several mixed-use developments like Meta's

Willow Village. The huge catch-up projects from Meta and Google, intended to alleviate their affordable-housing problems, seem to assume that tech workers care more about their work environment than they do about their home environment. The assumption seems to be that free food, complimentary laundry, and discounts at company stores will attract talent, even if that talent must contend with difficult commutes, undersized and expensive housing, expensive daycare, and less-desirable education choices for their children. The COVID-19 experience, which forced so many workers to make their home environment double as their work environment, was viewed by many workers as a possible improvement to the traditional day at the office. Of course, Meta and Google can afford the luxury of ideas like the Willow Village mixed-use development not producing the needed results, but smaller companies in less glamorous locations have less tolerance for failing to deliver cost-effective results.

A recent article in the *Wall Street Journal* entitled "Behold, The New Starting Salary for Some Graduates Is $100,000" highlights the pressure employers are feeling to pay much higher starting salaries at big tech, finance, and consulting firms. The article also talks about the resentment of more experienced employees at these firms as they see pay for new recruits jump by large amounts. It can be difficult to identify with the housing problems of employers like Google, Meta, Goldman Sachs, Citicorp, and McKinsey. It is also hard to shed tears for the new college graduates being forced to get by on six-figure starting salaries, but this relatively small group of workers who now have increasing bargaining power with some of the most powerful employers is a significant change. This change seems to support the work done by Charles Goodhart and is explained in his 2020 book *The Great Demographic Reversal*. Mr. Goodhart's theory is that a long glut of inexpensive labor has kept prices down for decades, but the deflationary forces of the last thirty to forty years are now giving way to an era of worker shortages. He believes the COVID-19 pandemic will mark the dividing line between deflation and resurgent inflation for the next two decades. He predicted that inflation in advanced economies will settle at 3 to 4 percent around the end of 2022 and remain at that level for decades. This compares to inflation of about 1.5 percent experienced in the decade before the pandemic. It is interesting to note how much more accurate Mr. Goodhart's 2020 inflation forecast has been than the forecast in 2021 by Fed officials, who projected that inflation would recede to 2.1 percent by the end of 2022. Private fore-casters surveyed by the *Wall Street Journal* in 2021 projected 2.4 percent by the end of 2022. These forecasters had increased their end-of-year estimate to 4.8 percent by the summer of 2022 and the Fed had doubled its estimate, saying its 2 percent target is unlikely before 2025.

Simply put, Mr. Goodhart points out that the working-age popu-lation has started shrinking across advanced economies for the first time since World War II, combined with declining birth rates. As labor becomes scarcer, workers will demand higher wages. Businesses will manufacture and invest more locally to offset both labor shortages and globalized supply chain problems, resulting in increasing production costs and increasing worker bargaining power. Global savings will decline as older people consume more than they produce, especially regarding healthcare. Labor shortages in man-ufacturing, the restaurant industry, leisure, and retailing are also resulting in wage pressure for small businesses. The fights for a higher minimum wage and the attempts starting to succeed for unionization at companies like Starbucks and Amazon attract less dramatic media coverage but will deliver far more impact to the U.S. economy.

An August 2023 article in the *Wall Street Journal* entitled "Striking L.A. Workers Want Hotels to Help Build Affordable Housing" shows that workers are beginning to look to their employers for affordable housing relief. Unite Here Local 11 represents 15,000 cooks, housekeepers, dish-washers, front-desk attendants, and other hospitality workers in Southern California. Union leaders say soaring housing costs have eaten away previ-ous wage increases and they want the hotel industry to address the problem. In addition to an $11 an hour wage increase over 3 years, they are demanding employers institute a 7 percent fee or similar government tax to build homes affordable to hotel workers. In the Los Angeles metro area, median monthly rents increased to $2,100 in 2022 and a worker in Los Angeles County would need to make $43 an hour to afford a typical two-bedroom apartment. The current minimum hourly wage for Unite Here Local 11 workers is $19 an hour. Hotel owners say fixing the region's housing crisis isn't their job and negotiations were suspended in July of 2023. This will be an interesting negotiation to follow as Los Angeles prepares to host the 2026 World Cup and the 2028 Summer Olympics.

Employers who entertain the concepts of labor hoarding and reject the idea of disposable employees who can be easily replaced when good times return, find truth in a statement by Professor Jefferey Pfeffer of the Stanford Graduate School of Business, who stated in a December 2022 article in *The Guardian* entitled "Heartless mass layoffs hit U.S. workers ahead of holidays," by Michael Samato. Professor Pfeffer said, "Layoffs are basically a bad decision."

Labor hoarding is an old idea gaining new popularity with employers who realize that good employees are their most important assets. These employers believe in investing more in their employees in times of economic downturn to avoid re-hiring and training costs when economic conditions improve. They are also conscious of the fact that studies have found that a layoff is one of the most stressful life experiences and is correlated with serious physical and mental health problems. In addition, even small layoffs can damage the morale of employees who are not affected, but are left with the question: *Am I next?* Although the 61,900 laid-off employees in 2022 in the major tech companies referenced above are only a small slice of current and expected job cuts in the tech world, they represent uprooting the lives of 61,900 individuals and families. It has been estimated that since 2022 layoff tallies at all tech companies have reached nearly 300,000 workers.

In a *New York Times* article dated October 12, 2022, the owners of Fat Daddy's Pizzeria and Bistro Provenance in Provo, Utah, tell the story of owners whose business plan is aimed at avoiding firing employees at all costs. These owners explained that they would choose to cut hours, take pay cuts themselves, and fire employees only as a last resort in the event of a major decline in business. At about the same time, one of Silicon Slopes' unicorns, purchased in 2014 for $3.8 billion, announced it was laying off 400 workers and moving those jobs to India. That company's average pay for those workers was about $80,000, and the severance pay, and medical coverage was a matter of weeks. The manager who made the "so sorry" announcement said the layoffs were based on a "challenging economic climate." I believe it is far more likely that I will be dining at Fat Daddy's Pizzeria than doing business with the company now transferring jobs to India when the new upturn arrives. To show that the restaurant owners' plan has confirmation from some leaders in the tech world who have a somewhat similar leadership style in 2023, Apple CEO Tim Cook, who made $99.4 million in 2022, suggested he take a $50 million pay cut in 2023. $50 million is a very small percentage of Apple's profits, but it shows that he is willing to think beyond his immediate interests and consider what's best for Apple. In addition, that decision earns him a lot of credibility with employees and shareholders as Apple faces supply chain disruptions and other challenges in 2023.

It would also be a mistake to think of this changing wage landscape as being only a U.S. problem. In China, where the workforce is expected to shrink by about 100 million workers over the next fifteen years, Chinese companies are already absorbing higher costs and wages by reducing profit margins. In Germany, labor shortages are so acute that the government is seeking to attract about 400,000 skilled foreigners a year. As the evidence shows, the U.S. and other advanced economies are entering an era of worker shortages and now have capital to retain and compete for the workers they need. Examples like Meta's Willow Village inform us that competing for the needed workers is more expensive and more difficult than expected. In Austin, Texas, Tesla, and Google alone were planning to hire 15,000 new workers in the coming quarters, with wages between $200,000 and $1 million per year. Of course, the events since mid-2022 may modify those forecasts.

As I was examining these large and rapidly growing employer/employee problems in the U.S. and internationally, I was interrupted by similar problems in my hometown. I live in a resort community of about 9,000 residents, where its many wealthy citizens are starting to realize that housing is now so expensive that schoolteachers, police officers, hotel workers, and restaurant workers cannot afford to live in or near city limits. Recently, doctors and other medical staff for our world-class hospital were added to that list. Vail Resorts, owner of one of my community's major ski resorts, was recently engaged in a protracted negotiation with its ski patrollers regarding its $15 an hour minimum wage rate for entry-level patrollers. These seasonal employees were asking for $17 an hour. After finally agreeing to that increase, Vail Resorts experienced a difficult ski season in 2021–2022, primarily due to staffing problems. In March of 2022, Vail Resorts announced an increase in the minimum wage for all seasonal employees to $20 an hour with some positions, including ski patrollers, receiving a $21 minimum wage. This change will apply to all thirty-seven of Vail's properties in North America. This new minimum wage is expected to impact smaller community businesses that compete with Vail for seasonal workers. At the same time, Vail made an increased commitment to affordable housing for its employees. Despite missing the quarterly earnings estimate, Vail Resorts' stock rose strongly after the announcement. Perhaps hotel owners in Los Angeles should look into what Vail has done to solve its staffing problem.

CHAPTER 5

HOMELESSNESS

A S STATED IN THE INTRODUCTION, AFFORDABLE housing is defined as housing that does not take more than 30 percent of an owner's pre-tax income to pay the sum of mortgage payments, property taxes, and insurance or more than 30 percent of a renter's pre-tax income to pay rent. The homeless are largely a population without income or incomes so undependable that employers, including the government, do not consider them a labor resource. By definition, the homeless problem is not really a housing-affordability problem. The homeless problem must be addressed by the government and by charitable and religious organizations. Some portion of the homeless population can be raised to levels leading to employment in situations such as successfully addressing medical problems, substance abuse problems, illiteracy, or lack of language skills, but some conditions, such as old age, incurable physical or mental problems, and lack of family support will prevent a large portion of the homeless from working out of poverty through free-market employment.

That said, homelessness is a huge and rapidly growing problem. The National Low Income Housing Coalition estimates there is a shortage of 7 million homes for the poorest renters in the U.S. Before 1992, housing readiness was the dominant model for dealing with this problem. It required those who needed housing to meet a list of stability requirements in order to qualify for housing. In 1992, Pathways to Housing pioneered the Housing-first model in New York City, which saw housing as integral to tenant recovery, not as a reward for achieving it. Salt Lake City, Utah, was among the first large cities in the U.S. to adopt the housing-first model in 2005 and was recognized in 2014 for its success. Backed by Salt Lake City mayor Erin Mendenhall, the first tiny home in a new tiny-house community on a thirty-seven-acre parcel in city limits was announced in August 2022 and is being spearheaded by the non-profit Other Side Academy. A 280-square foot unit is the first of sixty units and was designed by graduate students in the University of Utah Architecture School with a unit cost of roughly $90,000. Construction of this initial unit started in May 2022 and was completed in early August. This tiny-home community is targeted at the homeless population and requires the Salt Lake City Council to approve a public benefits analysis and a rezoning request for the site. Buildout is expected to be in stages and take several years, with total project cost estimated to be $7.5 million. The site cost is made possible by a discounted lease on the thirty-seven-acre city-owned land.

In 2021, Utah had 9.8 homeless individuals per 10,000 residents (about 3,565 people), a lower rate than other western states. California had a 2021 rate of 40.9 homeless individuals per 10,000 residents. Utah's homeless system spent more than $100 million in 2017 on direct and indirect costs associated with the homeless, and by 2019 that figure had increased to more than $300 million. The number of unsheltered individuals in Utah has grown by nearly 200 percent since 2016, while the number of sheltered individuals has only decreased by 6 percent. A recent legislative audit found that Utah's strategy to tackle homelessness estimated the cost of permanent supportive housing to be about $250,000 to $275,000 per unit. One result of that approach seems to be low turnover, with a high percentage of residents staying for ten years or more. Because few residents move on to more independent forms of housing, few new spaces are made available in existing facilities. In the next three years, Utah is expected to lose 4,000 affordable units as leases expire. A large percentage of those properties will be sold, remodeled, and listed at unaffordable prices. If Utah's rate of homeless individuals increases to the rate seen in California and some other western states, this problem will become politically unsustainable in Utah.

In 2022, Utah's governor recommended $128 million for projects to house the homeless, but the legislature agreed to fund only $55 million. That amount will be awarded through a grant process to developers of deeply affordable housing. At a time when the Utah legislature is sitting on a very large budget surplus and has received hundreds of millions of dollars in federal pandemic aid, this response to the homeless problem has been disappointing to Utah anti-poverty advocates. Disappointment continues. In its 2023, $29 billion budget, the Utah legislature prioritized a little over $198 million in new spending on various housing and homelessness programs. Utah lawmakers largely favored a freer market approach to deal with housing problems, and focused on getting out of developers' way so they could build more homes at more-effective price points. The legislature also stated that they were "balancing local control," which translated, means spot zoning. This new approach could allow a major development in my county to proceed without county approval. These state decisions make it difficult to know how much of the $198 million will be directed to the homeless problem or how the legislature will deal with the citizen and local government uproar over the spot zoning bills passed in 2023.

What many consider an inadequate response to a rapidly growing problem may be at least partially attributable to the Trump administration's Council of Economic Advisors turning negative to the housing-first model and growing criticism from think tanks like the Manhattan Institute and the Heritage Foundation. Recent conservative backlash in New York City, San Francisco, and other high-cost cities is leading to punitive approaches that de-emphasize the need to fund tenant follow-up support services. In New York City, Mayor Eric Adams announced a plan that could allow homeless individuals with mental illness to be involuntarily hospitalized. A new law in Missouri criminalizes sleeping outside on state-owned land.

The Biden administration has renewed federal support for housing in the American Rescue Plan, which has not gone unnoticed even in the very red state of Utah. In addition to examples like Houston, where a well-run housing-first program has moved more than 25,000 people into housing over the past ten years, another example gaining attention is the housing-first program established in 2008 to help homeless veterans. Housing vouchers for veterans provided by HUD were combined with case management and clinical services provided by the VA. The result has been that homelessness among veterans has declined by 55 percent since 2010.

In Utah, it would be worthwhile to focus on reducing the stick-and-bricks component of per-unit permanent supportive housing cost (the discussion in Chapter 14 regarding Boxabl homes may inform that suggestion). Improved building technology making possible faster delivery of high quality, relocatable, cost-effective housing combined with expanded tenant-support services through cooperation with Utah's strong health care providers may be the justification politicians need to provide adequate funding to solve the homeless problem.

In Nevada, Hope Springs, a homeless program in Reno estimates that it costs $36,000 a year in taxpayer and private funds to deal with a single homeless person compared to $15,000 a year to provide supportive housing to that person.

CHAPTER 6

THE PROBLEM WITH DEBT

THERE ARE AN ESTIMATED 79.36 MILLION OWN-
er-occupied homes in the U.S. and 62 percent of U.S. homeowners in
2020 had a mortgage. According to Rocket Mortgage, the average down
payment in America is equal to 6 percent of the borrower's loan value, and
it is possible to go down to as little as 3 percent. The growing homeowner/
renter net worth gap discussed in Chapter 2 has been a huge incentive for
new home buyers to use maximum leverage in buying homes, particularly
in recent times of mortgage interest rates near all-time lows.

New homeowners choosing to use maximum leverage to purchase
their new home do not usually stay in that home for the thirty-year or
fifteen-year life of the loan. Between 2000 and 2009, the average homeownership duration ranged from four to eight years and reached ten years by
2019. The pandemic and older Americans aging in place resulted in a peak
of 13.4 years in 2020, which has only fallen to 12.3 years in 2023. Only about
37 percent of Americans have lived in their homes for more than ten years.

Homeownership duration is very important to highly leveraged
homeowners due to the current system of home finance. Lenders por-
tray themselves as the good guys who make it possible for ordinary people to achieve the American dream of home ownership. Banks, mortgage

companies, credit unions, and many other lenders assure us that the banking transgressions associated with the 2008 recession and the government bail-out that followed are a thing of the past. Today these lenders have a great amount of control over what is built, who builds it, and who buys it. The typical home purchase by the average buyer utilizing a thirty-year mortgage requires a down payment and closing fees, followed by front-weighted mortgage loan payments for the life of the loan. This results in most of the equity buildup occurring in the final seventeen years of the homeowner's thirty-year mortgage. The home equity numbers for homeowners now so envied by renters striving to join the owner group are primarily based on the home-price appreciation they see in their location of interest. Once the renter succeeds in attaining home ownership, he becomes a cheerleader for rising home prices and an enthusiastic opponent of any neighborhood development that might have a negative impact on his new home. Although the new homeowner is now deeply in debt, he only sees headlines like those in the *Wall Street Journal* article in March of 2022, entitled "Homes Earned More for Owners Than Their Jobs Last Year," where Zillow stated that the increase in value of the typical U.S. home exceeded median worker incomes for the first time.

A change in personality that often comes with new home ownership is understandable because the new owner has entered into a contract with his lender that is heavily weighted toward protecting the lender from any possible negative event. The 5.7 million homes lost to foreclosure and short sale in the 2007 to 2011 period did result in some lender losses, but that damage was reduced by government bailouts; however, 100 percent of the home equity earned by those 5.7 million homeowners prior to 2007 was lost. Renters who never achieved home ownership suffered a related problem in the 2008 recession and later in the pandemic when their wages would not cover their rent. They had entered into a contract with their landlord that was heavily weighted toward protecting the landlord. Landlords needed that protection because in most cases, they, too, had a mortgage to pay.

As the negative outcomes of the 2008 recession fade and today's home-owners and renters hoping to become new homeowners once again believe in ever-increasing housing prices, they ignore the risks of home ownership, especially the risks of unaffordable home ownership.

Purchasing a highly leveraged home means, for most households, that their most important asset is also one of the least diversified assets you can own. This investment strategy is much like purchasing a large amount of stock in a single company that has no geographical diversification, no product diversification, and no earnings on 80 to 90 percent margin and is subject to unknown future maintenance expenses. You will be counting on being able to make 360 monthly payments in order to repay your loan in the hope that your capital gains after taxes will fund a comfortable retirement. That plan might have been a home run for early investors in Apple but would probably not be recommended by even the mortgage lenders for residential real estate.

In today's world of rapidly rising home prices and volatile interest rates, it is easy to forget that lender returns are much more assured than any speculative gains accruing to residential property owners. Lender returns are also more significant than the relatively small profits or fees earned by those involved in construction, marketing, legal services, and government services and taxes—expenses you pay even if you pay cash for your home. The obvious problem with debt is that you must pay it back. Charlie Munger offered some good advice when he said, "Three things ruin people: drugs, alcohol, and leverage."

CHAPTER 7

PROFITEERING LANDLORDS

I T WOULD BE A BIG MISTAKE TO BELIEVE THAT VERY smart people have not found what they consider to be the answer to affordable housing. Unfortunately, that answer is not to the question of how to reduce or eliminate the affordable-housing problem, rather it is to how to control and profit from this problem.

In the aftermath of the 2008 recession, private equity started buying foreclosed residential properties at big discounts by purchasing distressed mortgages being auctioned off by Fannie Mae and Freddie Mac. Homes obtained at large discounts were rented at prices that covered repairs, maintenance, and other carrying costs, leaving private equity to profit from rising home values. In 2013, Blackstone created a new financial instrument, a single-family rental securitization that proved very attractive to investors. By 2016, 95 percent of distressed mortgages had been auctioned off and private equity purchases moved to the open market. As prices rose and competition increased, Single-Family-Rental (SFR) expanded into Built-For-Rental (BFR) homes. An estimated 44,700 BTR houses are under construction in 2023 after BTR homes achieved the best return on investment (ROI) of all property sectors with risk-adjusted annual yields of more than 8 percent in the past two years. John Burns Real Estate Consulting has stated that more than $50 billion is flooding the single-family-rental market, up from just $3 billion in 2020. According to Redfin, real estate investors bought a record 18.4 percent of the homes sold in the U.S. during the fourth quarter of 2021, up from 12.6 percent a year earlier. Of the 80,293 homes purchased in that period by investors, 73.3 percent were paid for with all cash. $50 billion translates into 125,000 $400,000 single-family homes, but that number could be much larger if leverage is used. In an August 2022 article entitled "Everyone's a Landlord-Small-Time Investors Snap Up Out-of-State Properties," the *Wall Street Journal* discussed how recent technologies help so-called "laptop landlords" buy homes far from where they live. Online real estate marketplaces such as Roofstock and Appreciate provide listings and data enabling small investors to buy individual homes, often in other states, to rent out. These websites also connect investors to financing or local managers who can handle property maintenance and leasing.

According to CoreLogic, single-family-home purchases by investors have rose from 17 percent in February of 2019 to 28 percent in February of 2022, with small investors that own two to ten homes accounting for about half of all investor purchases. Purchases of just one home were excluded to rule out vacation homes. As a result, even small housing markets are becoming less local. For small investors, the article noted that landlord-friendly states are those where there are no limits on how much a renter can be asked to pay for a security deposit and where evictions are faster than other locations, together with a tolerance for other forms of renter abuse.

In popular resort communities, the one-home vacation-home purchases excluded from CoreLogic's data are often used for nightly rentals made possible by Airbnb and VRBO and have the same local impact of removing affordable housing or even affordable long-term rentals from those local citizens who work in town.

In order to continue extracting the ever-increasing short-term profits necessary to satisfy their investors, SFR and BFR operators will continue to increase rents, cut operating costs including maintenance costs, and impose ever-increasing tenant fees. A September 2023 *Wall Street Journal* article entitled "What's Worse Than Record High Rent? Record High Rent, Plus Fees" reports that the five largest single-family rental landlords increased their annual fee income per lease by about 40 percent between 2018 and 2021. That information was based on data from the House of Representatives Committee on Financial Services. Invitation Homes reported "other income" which includes fees, grew at more than twice the rate of rent in 2022, The record increase in rents now taking place nationwide adds a new dimension to the affordable-housing problem. Even those SFR and BFR landlords who avoid the whatever-the-market-will-bear theory of rent pricing and manage property care and tenant communication responsibly, will have to answer to their investors about ROI expectations. The growing captive audience who are finding they cannot afford to purchase the single-family or condominium lifestyle that has come to be known as the American Dream are now being asked to settle for renting that dream. As soaring rents increase much faster than wages, more tenants will be forced to shoulder cost-burdened rents or accept smaller, less-desirable housing alternatives. Renters at all price levels need relief from cost-burdened rents, and their employers are the answer. Chapters 11 through 14 will discuss a partnership between employers and their employees as a solution to this problem.

Since housing returns can only act as an inflation hedge for owners if cash flow from properties increases on par with inflation, the inflationary future forecast by Charles Goodhart discussed in Chapter 4 may not allow today's SFR/BFR housing dynamic to be sustainable in the not-too-distant future.

CHAPTER 8

LUXURY HOME SPECULATION

A JUNE 15, 2022, ARTICLE IN THE *WALL STREET JOURNAL'S* Real Estate section entitled "A Billionaire Bought a Florida Home for $94.2 million Last Year. Now He's Selling It for Around $175 million," is an extreme example of luxury residential real estate as an investment vehicle unrelated to the functional necessity of life that provides shelter for the 79 million families that occupy homes in the U.S. As ugly as this speculative frenzy by the 1 percent may seem to those experiencing the pain of increasingly burdened housing costs, it is not an affordable-housing problem. Today's version of "Lifestyles of the Rich and Famous" follows many historical Gilded Age examples and seems much closer to stock market speculation and investing in art and collectibles than to any comparisons with production housing.

I have met many luxury homeowners, and my experience is that the majority have been able to buy or build those homes as a result of success in building businesses, professional careers, or intelligent investments not related to residential real estate. Owning a luxury home is often a reward for the sacrifices of success but is not often the result of inheritance or luck and is almost never based on spectacular gains from starter homes.

It is difficult to understand why homeowners at all price levels enjoy long-established tax benefits, but equivalent benefits are not extended to renters. Tax benefits for employers who provide affordable housing for their employees may be a more efficient way to reach owner/renter tax parity. That complicated topic is a subject for another day, but for now the elimination of rent in excess of the 30 percent affordability standard is the most logical path to building renter equity.

In my hometown, the median sales price of single-family homes in August of 2023 was $3,587,500 and there were no detached single-family homes listed for sale under $1,000,000. The area bordering city limits showed a median sales price of $2,650,000 in that same month and there was one home listed for under $1,000,000.

In order to enjoy owning a luxury home, you must live in or near a community with excellent teachers, police and fire protection, city workers, restaurants and retail, doctors and nurses, and plumbers. The support and skills these people and many others provide is deteriorating rapidly as essential workers are forced to relocate in order to find affordable housing. A continued hollowing out of the workforce in our most desirable communities will hurt property values of luxury homes more than any problems concerning locating affordable housing near overly sensitive neighborhoods. Unlike homelessness, this is not a job for charity, but does require those with no affordable-housing problem to recognize and support the higher prices needed by employers to pay living wages for their employees. The example cited in Chapter 4 of Vail Resorts rethinking its initial opposition to raising its minimum wage and providing an increased commitment to affordable housing for its employees informs this point. Now, Vail's clientele, who include a substantial number of luxury homeowners, must recognize the value of paying more for their ski experience. They should also understand that other community businesses forced to meet Vail's wage increase do so in order to stay in business and maintain the community experience full-time residents, second homeowners, and visitors expect.

CHAPTER 9

THE PROBLEM OF TOXIC SOLUTIONS

AFFORDABLE HOUSING SOLUTIONS BROUGHT FOR-ward in the past to solve problems caused by inflation are a prime example of toxic solutions. The cost of shelter accounts for 40 percent of the core Consumer Price Index (CPI). Rent controls brought on by World War I and II bloomed in the inflationary spiral of the 1970s. Now, a new post-pandemic wave of inflation has captured the financial headlines and is reviving interest in rent-control legislation. It seems to be forgotten that rent-control enthusiasm was short-lived in the 1970s as lawmakers came to see rent controls as hurting housing markets more than they helped tenants by discouraging new development and disincentivizing apartment mainte-nance. Many states passed laws to prevent local governments from writing their own rent rules. More than two-dozen states have other prohibitions, with a number of rent control measures banned long ago in statewide ref-erendums. Today, rents are exploding at a pace far faster than income and in many of the states where rents are rising rapidly, more than 50 percent of renters are cost-burdened, spending more than 30 percent of their income on rent. With national rents up over 14 percent year-to-year in 2022 and rent control caps in legislation being proposed ranging from 2 to 10 percent, it seems we are headed into the same old fight with the same old combatants, which will lead to the same old lack of results. In November of 2021, voters in St Paul, Minnesota, enacted a new rent-control law that limits yearly rent increases to 3 percent and applies that limit to new construction buildings and vacant apartments. According to Real Page, a property management software firm, local builders and developers in St. Paul soon placed more than a third of planned apartment units on hold after the rent-control law was passed.

It has been said that insanity is doing the same thing over and over again but expecting different results. This points to the basic problem of toxic solutions: Beating dead horses like rent control wastes the time and efforts of people genuinely interested in solving the problem of affordable housing. Recent efforts by the Federal Reserve to rely on forty-year-old strategies to fight inflation in the much-changed world of today may also produce unexpected results (banking problems come to mind). Paul Volker's aggressive assault on the inflation of the late 1970s and early 1980s pushed short-term interest rates to just short of 20 percent and sent unemployment to nearly 11 percent in 1981. Inflation reached a peak of 14.6 percent in 1980. The Fed was telling us, until recently, that small rate hikes would deliver the economy from a similar scenario and return the inflation rate to the 2-percent target. This forecast assumed that the effects of the current wage-price spiral and oil price increases rooted in geopolitical instability would be easily controlled by these smaller steps taken much earlier in the inflationary cycle. Now, the periodic rate hikes have become larger with the inflation rate plateauing at higher levels and resisting declines to the Fed's target levels.

The 140,000 members of the National Association of Home Builders have released a three-pronged affordable solution that urges first a reduction of burdensome regulations that account for nearly 25 percent of the price of building a single-family home and more than 30 percent of the cost of multifamily development. The second recommendation is to suspend tariffs on Canadian softwood lumber and negotiate a new long-term lumber agreement. Lastly, they demand immediate remedies to lumber and building material supply chain bottlenecks. These three core problems are not candidates for quick resolution and, turbocharged by rising interest rates, inflationary pressure, and steadily rising wages, they make accurate forecasting impossible.

The last examples of the problem of toxic solutions come from Salt Lake City, where in late 2019, city leaders hoping to encourage the construction of more affordable housing introduced the affordable-housing overlay—zoning changes meant to reduce barriers and entice more infill and redevelopment on existing properties. The goal was for new apartments, townhomes, cottages, row houses, and similar dwellings to be built in what are now neighborhoods of single-family homes. Permitted density changes to allow additional building height, smaller setbacks, and reduced parking requirements per home, as well as fast-tracking city hall reviews were some aspects of the plan. In exchange for these benefits, property owners and developers would be required to set aside 20 percent of resulting new homes for rent subsidies for those making less than 80 percent of the city's median income. The envisioned rents were $1,400 per month.

All aspects of this plan were soon being protested and criticized in public hearings from residents from five community councils in what are some of Salt Lake City's oldest single-family neighborhoods. A common theme of protestors is that the construction encouraged under the affordable-housing overlay would fragment and even destroy the character of these communities, lower property values, and worsen problems with on-street parking. Some residents pointed out that these beautiful neighborhoods, largely built in the 1920s to 1940s, were some of the best planned and well-thought-out subdivisions of their time and have been maintained and remodeled at the highest level ever since. They also pointed out that the $1,400 a month rental target did not meet the 30 percent of monthly income standard for many area residents. Residents also complained that existing rules against short-term rentals listed on Airbnb or VRBO weren't being enforced, and some called for direct rent controls, which is prohibited by Utah state law.

In Chapter 2, it was pointed out that homeowners, and especially new homeowners, often protest any growth near their homes that they perceive as a threat to their accumulated home equity. Sometimes these protests are without merit, especially when the growth envisioned falls within existing development rules. The affordable-housing overlay, however, is an example of a toxic solution and is different because the local government planning change actually does harm the neighbors who have correctly pointed out its flaws. At the same time, the delay and expense of the approval process has contributed to making any developer's future project less than affordable for the intended occupants while likely not being financially viable for the developer.

More than two years ago, Ivory Homes, Utah's largest homebuilder started a project—The Capital Park Cottages—to develop 3.2 acres of open space in an older residential neighborhood that required a rezoning of the existing zoning first enacted in 1987. What followed was two years of debate and four versions of the hotly contested proposal, which would allow for a total of thirty-eight new dwellings, as well as robust opposition from hundreds of neighbors. The planners said that approximately ten dwellings per acre would be a change from very low density to low density. Neighbors were concerned about additional traffic and street safety, parking problems, loss of green space, air pollution, wildfire dangers, compressed setbacks, and feel that the large, two-story houses with four or five bedrooms and three-car garages will not be compatible with the neighborhood's older, smaller single-story homes that are less than half the size of the planned so-called cottages. They pointed out that the prices for the homes will likely exceed $1 million apiece and the built-in accessory units (ADUs) featured in many of the homes will be rented at market rates. Based on these facts, the protesting neighbors' position was that this is not affordable housing and will destroy the character of their neighborhood. In mid-December 2022, the Salt Lake City council approved the hotly contested rezone.

SECTION 2

A PATH TO A SOLUTION

The solution to the unfolding affordable-housing problem lies in a proper reading of history, dating back a century, combined with a recognition of a new housing dynamic that contains a simple flaw that can be corrected. A solution informed by these two lessons can solve the problems we face today in providing affordable housing for all workers. This solution is scalable but will take years to implement.

CHAPTER 10

HELP FROM THE PAST

Relevant Historical Information

Company towns, or more specifically, single-enterprise towns, were an old idea that attempted to solve the affordable-housing problem and almost succeeded more than a century ago. Company towns have a long history in the United States. By 1916, a thousand companies were providing housing for roughly 3 percent of the U.S. population—more than 60,000 employees. Some of these communities did well, like Corning, New York, and Hershey, Pennsylvania, while others like Gary, Indiana, did not. These company towns were either "exploitationville" or were built on a more utopian model.

The little-known Copperton community in Salt Lake County, Utah, was established in 1926 as a model city for its employees by the Utah Copper Company (UCC). In 1926, UCC was the dominant mining company in Utah and while other mining towns featured crowded streets, densely packed boarding houses, and other aspects not conducive to family life, UCC decided that a quality company town could be a showplace for homes that would advertise the advantages of copper building products. More importantly, it would contribute to recruiting and retaining the best workforce.

Copperton, which grew to more than 200 homes, was designed by one of Utah's leading architects and offered more than eighty-five variations for four-and five-room plans that were rented to employees for $22.50 and $27.50 per month, respectively. Homes and amenities were kept in good condition (regular cleaning, painting, and repairs) by the company, with yard maintenance the responsibility of the occupant. Due to the price and the quality of the homes, there were many more interested employees than there were houses, with strict priorities for allotting homes to key employees. If a worker retired or quit, he was no longer eligible for a home in the town. This proved an important competitive advantage for UCC and was the reason Copperton was able to defy the boom–bust cycle typical of Utah's mining towns.

After World War II and the takeover of Utah Copper Company by Kennecott Copper, Kennecott decided to get out of the housing business and sold all the homes in Copperton to private individuals in 1956. This historic company town survives today.

The Lessons of Copperton

The Copperton homes and community amenities were built with cash by a prosperous employer and rented to their employees at an attractive price. The Utah Copper Company controlled the wages of its employees and the cost of their housing. Balancing these two levers, UCC could ensure that employee housing was always affordable and always fully rented. As the owners and caretakers of the employee housing stock, UCC discovered that the 5 to 6 percent increase in costs due to the use of quality materials (including copper materials) was offset by savings in maintenance over a short number of years.

These kinds of outcomes are not surprising, but what is surprising is the company's understanding of the superior long-term profit potential of making quality employee housing available and affordable to their key employees. Other companies of the time were faced with similar circumstances, but opted to ignore or exploit their employees in good times and paid the price when hard times arrived. Companies that did not invest in quality housing or abandoned it in challenging times created conditions that resulted in employee dissatisfaction, leaving their workers only one course of action: To pressure their employers for higher wages or find a better-paying job. Companies that resisted that pressure in good times lost worker loyalty, but many employers could not meet demands for higher wages or even maintain payroll when the depression arrived. They had not made the investment that Utah Copper Company made and paid the price.

Why Company Towns Faded

Ironically, the historical facts that are most remembered by today's critics of company towns are the physical attributes of these communities. While the street plans, community amenities, home designs, and construction techniques pioneered between 1926 and 1956 were ahead of their time, they are not relevant today. Changes in society have made even the best company-town templates of the distant past unworkable in today's world. There is an enormous difference in the practicality of building a company town on vacant company-owned land with few neighbors and little government oversight, versus trying to shoehorn Willow Village into an already-dense community with traffic and infrastructure constraints, on super-expensive land surrounded by neighbors reacting to perceived threats to their own property.

Only a few of the current 800+ residents of Copperton work at the Bingham mine, which is now owned by Rio Tinto and is still one of the largest open-pit copper mines in the world. Roads and transportation advances have made clustering employees close to their work unnecessary. More attractive residential choices within easy commuting distance have long been available, and recently the pandemic experience has moved work out of the office and into the home.

It is also easy to see how living in a community comprised entirely of co-workers was better than the alternative in 1926, but while Willow Village's smaller apartments in four-story buildings may deliver more affordable living costs (those final costs are, as yet unknown), they fall short in terms of an acceptable lifestyle for a growing family in the long-term.

The physical attributes that made Copperton a visionary project long ago may have faded into obsolescence, but the real vision of the employers who built Copperton was their recognition that a partnership with the workers who were their most valuable asset required an investment in the lives and families of those workers.

CHAPTER 11

SOME CLUES FROM TODAY'S HEADLINES

THE RECENT SUCCESS ENJOYED BY SFR AND BFR companies and their investors is providing the blueprint to build an ever-increasing amount of residential real estate. The short-term ROI required to sustain that volume of housing construction requires rent increases that exceed worker wage increases. This fatal flaw, and the renter abuse it fosters, can be corrected by substituting the employers who pay those wages for the lenders, private equity firms, and investors who now profit from the affordable-housing problem.

Employers who choose to purchase or build residential housing for cash and enter into fifteen-year leases with their employees at rates not to exceed 30 percent of the employee's salary can eliminate the need for lenders and landlords.

- Employers acting as conservative, long-term investors would retain ownership of all purchased-for-rent and built-for-rent properties and assume all risk and reward related to future changes in market value.

- Regular wages offered in addition to the housing leases would be set below competitive salaries in the employer's market area, as shown in the Chapter 13 employer/employee partnership example.

- Employee salary increases would be limited to merit raises related to job performance, and cost-of-living raises would be eliminated. Any salary increases earned would result in rents being raised by 30 percent of the amount of the raise at the time of the raise, but the employee's housing cost would never exceed 30 percent of the employee's wages.

- By providing employees with the opportunity to match or exceed the equity build-up that would accrue to the purchaser of a comparable home with a 90 percent loan-to-value ratio, thirty-year mortgage as of the commencement date of the employer/employee partnership, the employer would eliminate down payments, closing costs, and carrying costs, including taxes and insurance costs (other than renters insurance), and even the loan application itself. This would make it possible for employees to use personal funds normally required for initial home ownership costs to establish equity through diversified investments of their choosing. This would answer the objections new residents have for opting out of home ownership, as discussed in Chapter 2.

- The recent surge in tech layoffs resulting from excessive hiring since the pandemic, as discussed in Chapter 4, and the common practice of last-in, first-out hiring make the risk avoidance offered by the employer/employee partnership a superior choice for new recruits versus the risks of undiversified property ownership, especially in the early years of an employee's career.

- This arrangement makes it optional for employee families to choose being a dual-income family, rather than a necessity needed to cover housing and child-care expenses.

- The various forms of renter abuse discussed in Chapter 2 would be addressed and prohibited in the employer/employee partnership agreement.

Chapter 12 will amplify the justification for the proposed employer/employee partnerships and explain further why existing employees and future recruits will see this arrangement as providing the major benefits of ownership without the problems of debt or renter abuse. Chapter 13 will offer a hypothetical example to better explain how the proposed employer/employee partnership could work, although endless modifications would be possible.

CHAPTER 12

WAKE UP, EMPLOYERS!
YOU HAVE A HOUSING PROBLEM

IF YOU BELIEVE THAT THE PROBLEMS FOR BUSINESS owners discussed in Chapter 4 are real and growing, now consider the proposition that the ideas presented in Chapters 10 and 11 might be combined to form a solution to the affordable housing problem. A further discussion of how employer/employee housing partnerships can loosen the Gordian Knot of affordable housing will help the reader evaluate the truth of this solution and which of Schopenhauer's three stages it deserves to occupy.

If the flaw in Wall Street's plan to maximize profits from the affordable-housing problem is continuing to charge rents that increase much faster than the wages of those who occupy their properties, how can that flaw be corrected? Simply put, the super landlords and even small-investor landlords must be replaced by the employers of those who are affected by the affordable-housing problem. Properly structured investments in residential real estate must take their place in the investment portfolios of profitable companies, from the largest to the smallest.

Rather than being solely a passive investor in the stock and bond markets, real estate securitizations, or collectibles, an employer could choose to devote a significant part of its company's investment portfolio to single-family rental housing for its current and future employees. The battle for the hearts and minds of the most talented and creative people who will shape every essential industry in the years to come will be fought outside the contest for best office and most office perks. The growing housing profits now flowing to lenders and private-equity landlords can instead flow to employer/employee partnerships. Employees will benefit from housing of superior quality that is guaranteed to remain free from renter abuse and guaranteed to cost no more than 30 percent of the employees' wages. Employers will benefit from long-term single-family home appreciation and savings from future employee wages being limited to merit raises. The direct involvement of company ownership is necessary in order to bypass the incentive structure of corporate managers. The current structure leads to managers assuming excessive risk, failing to undertake sufficient long-term investment, especially regarding research and development and employee recruiting and retention, and being overpaid based on the overemphasis on ROI tactics like stock buybacks.

By solving the affordable-housing problem for its employees, an employer can gain a competitive advantage over time by building a talented and loyal workforce, much like Utah Copper Company did a century ago. The alternative to taking on the responsibility for making sure the wages an employer pays will provide ongoing stability and happiness for workers and their families is to leave the most important company assets in the hands of lenders, landlords, and advisors with the hope that home buyer and renter abuse can be avoided or solved in some way other than continuing excessive increases in wages not tied to worker performance. Employers would not be competing with the lenders and landlords identified as sharing responsibility for the problem; rather, the employer's expanded role would eliminate the need for these people. The money saved can be shared with the employee in a way that changes a standard employment contract into a mutually beneficial partnership agreement.

Experienced, profitable business owners in any community have a deeper knowledge of those communities and the problems confronting their employees than do large, remote SFR and BFR operators and their investors or even smaller landlords. Capitalist competition rewards these advantages, just as it did in the early days of Copperton. Today's technology has made it possible to create virtual company towns. Rather than building a cluster of residences, as in historic company towns and in more modern versions like Meta's Willow Village, individual homes disbursed in the wider community and connected by the Internet offer much more flexibility for employers. The pandemic has demonstrated the flexibility of remote work and its advantages for workers. Although it is understandable that Apple, who opened a spectacular new $5 billion headquarters in Cupertino in 2019, would like to see it being used by Apple employees, the company's recent return-to-office rule encountered significant push-back from employees, who urged the executive team to consider a more flexible work schedule that emphasizes remote collaboration and eliminates the need for workers to commute. Shortly after that pushback, the company abruptly suspended its requirement that employees be in the office at least three days a week, citing a resurgence of COVID-19.

If Apple invested another $5 billion of their second quarter of 2022 $48 billion cash holdings in Bay-area median-priced single-family housing ($1,350,00 being the latest 2022 estimate of that cost), they could own 3,700 remote home-office locations, with the new headquarters acting as the mothership connecting thousands of satellite locations with Apple technology. That situation would seem to open endless new opportunities for what Apple does best. Since the rent from employees would not be tied to whatever the actual cost of housing built or purchased on the open market by Apple turned out to be, but rather would be tied to each employees' actual wages and set not to exceed 30 percent of total wages for the term of the partnership agreement, that employee's affordable-housing problem would be solved.

Building a diversified (by location and property type) portfolio of single-family rental homes as a cash buyer to be occupied by what would be ideal tenants would also contribute to success in recruiting and retaining top-talent employees and allow employers to control future wage increases. Among the many benefits for current and future employees, qualifying for employment with a participating company would eliminate qualifying with a lender for a mortgage loan and no down payment would be required. Home maintenance would not be the responsibility or an added expense for the occupant. There could also be an opportunity for the employee to build equity in the employer/employee partnership at a rate matching the equity build of a 90 percent loan-to-value, thirty-year fixed rate mortgage based on the appraised value of the home occupied at the thirty-year mortgage rate available at the partnership starting date. The company would retain ownership of the residential property and be responsible for major main-tenance. Future wage changes would not be guaranteed or forecasted, but rental credits and payments would be a constant percentage of wages paid to ensure that company-provided housing would never be unaffordable, that is, never above 30 percent of the employee's pre-tax income. The company would shoulder all the risk and reward for capital gains and losses associ-ated with the residential property but could guarantee an equity build-up earned by the tenant employee based on the original price of the home. This would be a powerful retention incentive, in addition to showing new recruits that they would build equity at a rate equal to purchasing a home of the same value. In the event the employee ceased to be employed by the company, the employee could be paid the full amount of the equity earned. The employment contract would enforce an even more utopian arrangement than the Copperton example, and it would protect employee tenants from all forms of renter abuse and whatever-the-market-will-bear rent increases. An example of a possible employer-employee partnership agreement will be included in Chapter 13 to provide more detail.

Although a logical choice for first-adopter targets to adopt the proposed solution would be some of the prosperous and growing tech companies, the nationwide affordable-housing problem is so widespread that the question of scalability must be considered. It is estimated that there are about 15,000 businesses in the U.S. with more than 1,000 employees, 215,000 businesses with 100 to 999 employees, and 1,140,000 businesses with twenty-five to ninety-nine employees. In Austin, Texas, Tesla, and Google alone were planning to hire 15,000 new workers in the near future with wages between $200,000 and $1,000,000 per year. In a market like Austin where housing supply is already limited, those hiring plans would likely result in extraordinary price increases for single-family and multifamily housing.

Warren Buffett was quoted as answering a question about his favorite time to sell assets with a one-word answer: "Never." I had a personal experience long ago that convinced me of the wisdom of Mr. Buffett's answer.

From 1993 to 1997, I was the managing partner in the development of a 126-unit single-family home project. The three-and four-bedroom homes on small lots ranged in size from 1778 to 3130 square feet and sold from $182,000 to $400,000. Profits were in the 6 percent range. In 2017, I looked at the sale of one of those homes—a 2523 square-foot, three-bedroom, three-bath, one-level home purchased by the original owner in 1997 for $235,000 and sold in October of 2017 for $925,000. If in 1997 I had the necessary funds and foresight to retain ownership of that home and rent it for 4 percent of market value, I would have received a gain of $668,000 in 2017 after collecting $464,000 in rental income, less $111,000 in property taxes at 1 percent of yearly market value and $60,000 in maintenance and repair costs at $250 per month. Based on my road-not-taken estimates, my total gain before capital gains and after commissions would have been $918,000. In the real world, I took my builder's profit of about $17,000 and moved on to the next home. Since I had not built the home out of pocket and the $218,000 (after commissions) was money owed with interest payments accruing daily, I had no other choice. That experience and 125 others that were very similar contributed to my diploma from the school of hard knocks.

To add to the pain, I later saw that the same home was sold by the 2017 buyer in November of 2020 for $1,350,000. I also noted that a 4 percent of value long-term rental rate based on the 2017 sales price would have resulted in a $3,083 per month rental rate (somewhat below the 2017 long-term market rental rate) requiring an annual salary of more than $123,000 to meet the 30 percent affordability standard. Based on the 2020 sales price, monthly rent would have increased to $4,467 per month, requiring annual household income of over $178,000 (close to the market rental rate). The 2020 buyer did a very nice remodel and sold the home in May of 2022 for $2,750,000. At that point, the home graduated from affordable, attainable housing to luxury housing.

Although we love to hear tales of homebuyers whose home purchase in the past was their ticket to a carefree retirement in the location of their dreams, that outcome is rare. I saw many different owners buy and sell homes in this project over the years and a few original owners remain, but owners who purchased just prior to the 2008 recession and were forced to sell in the immediate aftermath left with a different view of residential real estate speculation. The incredible growth and prosperity experienced in this location since the early 1990s was not matched by many small communities and is no guarantee of a similar future. A recent study by Zillow Group for the *Wall Street Journal* showed that in 477 U.S. cities, including Chicago, Cleveland, Hartford, and Detroit, the typical home value at the end of April 2022 was below peak levels from the early 2000s. Although these laggard cities represent only a fraction of the overall population, this study shows that for many homeowners, home-price appreciation in the next fifteen years is not a sure thing. I do know that these 126 production homes—built to be affordable for schoolteachers, single nurses, new families, and retired people—are now unaffordable for that demographic, both in terms of purchase and as long-term rental properties.

If the solution being offered requires many years to implement to a significant degree, how can it hope to have an impact in a reasonable period of time? The estimated 1,370,000 companies with more than twenty-five employees, plus another 4,780,000 firms with less than twenty-five employees, offer many opportunities to take small first steps in many places and a few big steps with large companies in highly competitive industries.

- If early implementations are successful in terms of recruiting success and profitability, this simple open-source idea (Schopenhauer's third stage) can spread rapidly among competitors. Each employer/employee situation is unique, so viral adoption and individual company customization can evolve at any pace.

- This is not a solution intended to save failing companies without resources, rather it is targeted at early adopters whose proof phase can be followed by the kind of dynamic growth seen in recent years in the SFR/BFR space. These early adopters can gain an expanding advantage over their closest competitors, who would then be under pressure to respond with similar tactics.

- Many of the 4,780,000 small business owners with less than twenty-five employees, especially those owned by minorities or women, say a key problem in being able to help their employees is their inability to pay their business rent. In a poll by Alignable of 7,331 randomly selected small business owners in August of 2022, 45 percent of those surveyed said their rent is at least 50 percent higher now than it was prior to the COVID-19 pandemic, 24 percent said rent is at least twice as high, and 12 percent said their rent is more than three times higher than it was before the pandemic. As a result, rent delinquency rates in August of 2022 were at 40 percent. Delinquency rates for minority-owned businesses were at 53 percent and 42 percent for women-owned firms. This data confirms the fact that the solution offered in this writing has severe limitations for less-successful small business owners, who may in extreme cases have a personal affordable-housing problem very similar to their workers'. Small businesses without the resources to help their workers secure affordable housing will lose out in future competition with more successful companies for needed workers. Businesses unsuccessful in retaining their existing workforce and attracting new workers will not remain viable in the future.

- The long-term benefit to the employer is not really an added cost, it is more a matter of an investment that can be considered as salary paid in advance in return for future salary control and major salary savings. Recruiting and retaining top quality employees versus just hiring more employees is the goal. This plan does not need to be force-fed to existing employees. In fact, the problem will be to manage the schedule of adoption by existing employees—the same problem Utah Copper Company encountered in building out Copperton.

- Other than the normal permitting process, this plan avoids the aggravation, unwise compromise, expense, and delay involved in securing entitlements for large, clustered projects that arouse residents and local government planners.

- This idea is compatible with many improvements now underway in home construction, like modular construction, energy efficiency, and smart-home technology. Companies working in these fields are modern-day pioneers, and they need early-adoption examples to prove the worth of what they produce. Just as UCC benefited from making homes in Copperton a showcase for copper building products, construction-technology companies could benefit from demonstrating and refining the value of their products.

- A company that encounters unexpected hard times in the future would hold assets that could be sold or used as collateral but could also be used to lessen the impact of those hard times on its employees. That flexibility is not provided by other investments such as stocks and bonds. The battle for tech talent is entering a new phase. The world's biggest tech companies have spent years battling with each other for engineers and other skilled workers. This battle extends to the rest of the tech landscape, especially the startups who use stock options to attract talent. This fierce competition makes sense because in tech, it's human capital that matters most. In 2022, rising interest rates and other market conditions are weakening growth-over-profits tech companies, while strengthening big tech companies who have amassed record amounts of cash. The recent cool down in recruiting top talent will help big tech companies hire better employees.

- As better employees see a musical-chairs scenario unfolding in the startup space, big tech should see increased opportunity to offer the best and brightest the safety employees will increasingly seek, and the ability to solve their housing-affordability problem would increase their flexibility in the coming bidding wars for attracting and retaining top talent. If remote work remains an important consideration in the tech world, particularly for dual-income households, that flexibility will be even more important in achieving results.

Just as companies come in all shapes and sizes, so do their employees. Apple has salaried engineers and executives, but also front-line store hourly workers. Engineers have been making news with their unhappiness with the company's plans to return to the office, but more recently Apple announced that starting pay for hourly workers in the U.S. would rise to $22 an hour (or higher) effective in July of 2022, ahead of the normal fall performance reviews. That $22 an hour rate is a 45 percent increase from 2018.

Apple's 2021 median compensation was $68,254, but that figure is $15,306 less than the annual compensation needed to purchase the $391,200 median prices home in the U.S. in May of 2022 (assuming a thirty-year mortgage at 5.5 percent with a $23,000 down payment to meet the 30 percent affordability standard). If that Apple employee can qualify for that loan and has the required down payment, he would be entering into a cost-burdened housing-affordability situation requiring more than 37 percent of their annual compensation to pay housing expenses. Of course, if Apple considers the fact that the median home price in the Bay area at that time was $1,350,000, reworking the affordability equation would require using the median compensation for all of the workers who are being required to spend two or three days a week working from the headquarters office in Cupertino.

The Labor Department released figures in April of 2022 that showed Apple's increased compensation budget was not the exception for U.S. businesses and government employers, who spent 4.5 percent more on worker wage costs in the first three months of 2022—the fastest rise since 2001. Since that increase exceeded the fourth quarter of 2021's annual growth, private-sector wages and salaries adjusted for inflation fell in the first quarter of 2022.

The specific housing needs of each employee are unique and present design challenges that must accommodate those needs. Housing location, initial construction cost, and ongoing maintenance costs are just some of the considerations that relate to product type. Single-family homes offer the most flexibility, but other choices are possible. A married couple with young children has needs that are different from an older couple with teenage children and single parents' needs can be different still.

- Workers who are disabled or caring for someone who is disabled, or an older extended family member may require disability modifications or one-level living.

- Employee spouses may need office or workspace if working from home.

- People are concerned for their pets and their hobbies and may consider outdoor living space important.

These are just a few of a long list of different challenges in solving the problem of what constitutes suitable housing, but they are the same problems builders and architects have been solving for custom and production home customers since long before Utah Copper Company built Copperton. Just as the architects from Scott & Welch and builders E.J. Teage and F.B. Bowers solved their problems with design variations and construction standardization more than ninety-seven years ago and continued to make improvements over time, the best builder–architect teams of today have the tools to do even better.

As discussed in Chapter 8, if you have workers who can afford luxury housing, they do not have an affordable housing problem and should not qualify for this program. These owners often have mortgages taken out for the tax benefits intended for ordinary homeowners, but not needed for ownership and full-time occupancy.

CHAPTER 13

THE EMPLOYER/EMPLOYEE PARTNERSHIP EXAMPLE

What Would Life Without Lenders and Profiteering Landlords Look Like?

The proposed solution would eliminate employee mortgage financing by substituting equity investment from their employer. Lenders would no longer have any control over what residential housing is built, who builds it, or who buys it. Recent experience shows that investors and wealthy buyers have already figured out that buying or building residential properties with all cash is a significant competitive advantage in any market with high prices and limited inventory. Employers would settle for the compounded historical rate of return for holding homes as long-term assets with no fixed sales date (remember, Warren Buffett's favorite holding period is forever). Employee rent would be set at 30 percent of the employee tenants' total pre-tax compensation to ensure that the employee never experiences an affordable housing problem. This example will show how an employer/employee partnership could be structured to guarantee housing affordability and wealth-building opportunities for employees while contributing to long-term employer profitability.

Let's look at a hypothetical example of how an employer/employee partnership agreement would work and how it could be used by employers to recruit and retain top talent.

Employee 1

Our hypothetical employer is an established major tech company operating profitably with cash assets that have been considered for conservative company investments or stock buybacks. Our hypothetical candidate for recruitment is married with two small children and has an outstanding resume to compete for jobs in the employer's location paying in the range of $90,000 to $110,000 a year. The candidate and his family now live in another state but are looking to relocate. After some initial discussions, you learn that the candidate and his wife do have some student-loan debt and are concerned for their children's education. The family was attracted to your location by the business climate and the personal recreation opportunities.

Your offer is annual compensation of $70,000. Your company will also purchase a $700,000 single-family home for cash with the obligation to pay all property taxes, maintenance and repair costs, and insurance. The employment contract will include a fifteen-year rental agreement for the home at a rate of $1,750 a month or $21,000 a year ($70,000 x 30 percent). Any merit raises during the fifteen-year term of the lease would increase rent by an amount equal to 30 percent of the raise at the time of the raise. In addition, you will provide an equity account that will duplicate the equity build that would result from a 90 percent, thirty-year fixed rate-mortgage loan at the current interest rate available at the signing date of the partnership agreement (assume a 7 percent interest rate) for the first fifteen years of the thirty-year mortgage loan. Your company would continue to be the owner of the home and incur all risk related to future changes in market value. Some important advantages for the tenant employee would be:

- No future rent increase other than those related to merit increases in the employee's compensation.

- An employee leaving the company would receive the total amount of his housing equity account.

- The company could allow certain withdrawals from that equity account to repay student loans, family medical expenses not covered by insurance, or family education expenses.

- As an employee tenant, our candidate will avoid any down payment and closing costs on the home.

Now, let's assume our candidate accepts your offer of employment after investigating competing offers. We can jump ahead five years and look back on his partnership results to see if both of you made a wise decision.

Five-Year Partnership History — Employee #1

Year	Employee compensation	Annual principal reduction on a $630,000, thirty-year fixed mortgage loan at 7%	Cumulative principal reduction from column 2	Employee's annual rent (30% of column 1)	Employee's monthly rent (column four divided by twelve)
1	$70,000	$6,400	$ 6,400	$21,000	$1,750
2	75,000	6,862	13,261	22,000	1,875
3	82,000	7,358	20,620	24,600	2,050
4	88,000	7,890	28,520	26,700	2,225
5	100,000	8,461	36,971	30,000	2,500

Employer's Five-year Partnership History

	End of year appraised value (assuming a $700,000 purchase price with 5% yearly appreciation)	Yearly appreciation (compounded at 5%)	Yearly gross rental income	Less annual carrying cost (pre-tax)	Less annual contribution to employee's partnership balance	Net rental income plus unrealized capital gains (columns 2 through 5)	Annual return (column 6 as a percentage of $700,000 purchase price)
1	$735,000	$35,000	$21,000	$ 9,000	$ 6,400	$ 40,600	(5.80%)
2	771,750	36,750	22,500	9,000	6,862	43,388	(6.20%)
3	810,337	38,587	24,600	9,000	7,358	46,831	(6.69%)
4	850,854	40,517	26,700	9,000	7,890	50,327	(7.19%)
5	893,396	42,543	30,000	10,000	8,461	54,082	(7.73%)

Why Your Offer Proved Beneficial for Both Parties

Our candidate investigated buying a comparable home to the one you offered as a rental. He learned that a $700,000 single-family home purchase utilizing a 90 percent (LTV), thirty-year fixed-rate mortgage loan required a $70,000 down payment plus significant closing costs, followed by $4,225 in monthly mortgage payments and carrying costs of about $9,000 a year. He learned that lenders were not anxious to make the required cost-burdened loan to a newly employed, relocating family without a large second paycheck from Mrs. Recruit or a much higher down payment or other collateral. The couple discussed the possibility of proceeding as a dual income family but found that solution inadequate and unacceptable based on their young children.

An investigation into renting a comparable single-family home, condominium, or apartment found rates far in excess of the $1,750 per month you offer, with ongoing additional fees and subject to future rent increases based on the whatever-the-market-will-bear theory.

The employee and his family were pleased with their decision to accept your offer, and he turned out to be a high-value employee who earned a number of merit raises that increased his annual salary to $100,000 in year #5; however, family circumstances forced him to leave at the end of year number five. You are sorry to see him go. His last check is for the $36,971 balance in his partnership equity account, and you wish him well.

Employee 2

You now need to hire a replacement and confirm that salaries now range between $120,000 and $130,000 a year for similar positions and experience in your market. You also find that homes comparable to the ones just vacated sell for $900,000 or more and mortgage rates have fallen to 4 percent for thirty-year fixed rate loans.

You find an outstanding replacement candidate and offer her a compensation package consisting of a $100,000 annual salary and a fifteen-year rental agreement at a rate equal to 30 percent of her $100,000 salary ($2,500 per month). The offer also includes the fifteen-year partnership equity account to equal the equity buildup that would accrue to a buyer of the home with a thirty-year, 90 percent LTV mortgage loan at 4 percent.

Our new candidate is a single parent with two teenage children relocating from another state. As she learns more about your company and the area, she finds that the purchase of a $900,000 home would require monthly mortgage payments of $3,867 with a $90,000 down payment plus closing costs. You also know that she has an offer from one of your competitors with a $125,000 starting salary. Her challenge would be to qualify for and maintain a cost-burdened loan of at least 37 percent of her salary, and the required down payment would require a large share of her savings. She also finds renting a comparable property much more expensive than the $2,500 rent you offer.

Using any conservative salary-increase estimates she would expect to achieve over the next five years, you can show her what your offer would yield.

Five-Year Partnership Forecast — Employee #2

Year	Forecast employee compensation	Annual principal reduction on a $810,000, thirty-year mortgage loan at 4% (years 1 through 5)	Cumulative principal reduction from column 2	Employee's annual rent (30% of column 1)	Employee's monthly rent (column 4 divided by twelve)
1	$100,000	$14,264	$14,264	$30,000	$2,500
2	100,000	14,844	29,108	30,000	2,500
3	108,000	15,451	44,559	32,400	2,700
4	108,000	16,080	60,639	32,400	2,700
5	117,000	16,735	77,374	35,100	2,925

Employer's Partnership History
Years Six through Ten

	End of year appraise value	Yearly appreciation (compounded d at 5%)	Yearly gross rental income	Less annual carrying cost (pre-tax)	Less annual contribution to employee's partnership balance	Net rental income plus unrealized capital gains (columns 2 through 5)	Annual return (column 6 as a percentage of $700,000 purchase price)
6	$ 938,065	$44,669	$30,000	$10,000	$14,264	$50,405	(7.20%)
7	984,918	46,903	30,000	10,000	14,844	51,560	(7.37%)
8	1,034,216	49,248	32,400	10,000	15,451	56,197	(8.03%)
9	1,085,926	51,711	32,400	11,000	16,080	57,031	(8.15%)
10	1,140,222	54,296	35,100	11,000	16,735	61,661	(8.81%)

Moving Forward in 2034

As only happens in hypothetical examples, the forecast you made in 2028 turned out to be 100 percent accurate and now you are in 2034, confronted with a new employee challenge. Employee 2 has exhibited outstanding performance and leadership ability. Her children have gone off to college (thanks to her partnership equity account) and you offer her a new position that involves opening a new territory for your company in another state. The new position will require extensive travel and the home originally purchased for $700,000 is no longer a good fit.

In preparation for her relocation, you begin a search for a suitable home in her new location. Mortgage rates have risen to 9 percent and the resulting recession has made 2034 an excellent time to be a cash buyer.

After a number of experiences since 2023 similar to your success with Employees 1 and 2, you have continued to build your employee force using the employer/employee partnership plan. Even though the recession has affected new hiring in 2034, you have not been able to meet the demand for the employer/employee plan from long-time employees, many of whom predate Employees 1 and 2. Several of these employees are excellent candidates for the soon-to-be-available home, and several plan to sell their existing homes, but are finding selling for appraised value difficult under current economic conditions. This opens the possibility of paying cash for existing employee homes suitable for conversion to an employer/employee partnership situation. In any case, you have interest in the original home purchased for $700,000 in 2023 and appraised for $1,140,000 in 2034.

You select the employee who best fits the home and move forward with a new forecast as follows (spoiler alert, it too turns out to be 100 percent accurate in 2039).

Five-Year Partnership Forecast — Employee #3

Year	Employee compensation	Annual principal reduction on a $1,020,000, 30-year fixed mortgage loan at 9% (a 90% LTV on the original home now appraised at $1,140,000)	Cumulative principal reduction from column 2	Employee's annual rent (30% of column 1)	Employee's monthly rent (column 4 divided by twelve)
1	$117,000	$6,968	$ 6,968	$35,100	$2,925
2	126,000	7,622	14,590	37,800	3,150
3	126,000	8,337	22,927	37,800	3,150
4	136,000	9,120	32,047	40,800	3,400
5	136,000	9,975	42,022	40,800	3,400

Employer's Partnership History
Years Eleven through Fifteen

Year	End of year appraised value (assuming a $700,000 purchase price with 5% yearly appreciation)	Yearly appreciation (compounded at 5%)	Yearly gross rental income	Less annual carrying cost (pre-tax)	Less annual contribution to employee's partnership balance	Net rental income plus unrealized capital gains (columns 2-5)	Annual return (column 6 as a percentage of $700,000 purchase price)
11	$1,197,233	$57,011	$35,100	$11,000	$6,968	$74,143	(10.59%)
12	1,257,095	59,862	37,800	11,000	7,622	79,040	(11.29%)
13	1,319,950	62,855	37,800	12,000	8,337	80,318	(11.47%)
14	1,385,948	65,998	40,800	12,000	9,120	85,678	(12.24%)
15	1,455,245	69,297	40,800	12,000	9,975	88,122	(12.59%)

This example is intended to be a reasonable guess as to future relative prices. It is not provided as a forecast, but only to illustrate the advantages of the two levers that Utah Copper Company discovered a century ago. By heeding Warren Buffett's advice that his favorite holding period is forever, residential real estate can become the key to recruiting and retaining the best workforce. Offering affordable housing combined with being a responsible landlord who does not exploit his employee tenants completes the solution. Residential real estate becomes a home for the employee and frees up their financial resources to build wealth in the stock market, non-residential real estate, or entrepreneurial pursuits. The same residential real estate becomes a conservative non-leveraged, long-term, diversified asset for the employer. It also provides an insurance policy against the unknowns of labor availability, remote working environments, and worker wage dissatisfaction.

Although this example is pure fiction, the numbers are based on realistic costs for one imagined future. In that fifteen-year journey into the future with one home purchased for $700,000 in 2023 and occupied by three employee tenants for five years each, many assumptions were made and the benefits that accrue to both the employer and the employer's three employees are as follows:

- The employer saves $329,000 in salary costs by offering lower salary plus an attractive fifteen-year lease to his employee tenants.

- The tenant lease payments provide a positive cash flow of $165,000 from the three five-year leases.

- The home purchased in 2023 appreciates by $755,000 (pre-tax) over fifteen years.

Total employer benefit: $1,249,000

Employee benefits:

- The three employees receive quality, affordable housing that never costs more than 30 percent of their total compensation.

- They receive employee equity account payments totalling $156,000 over fifteen years. These payments are equal to the equity buildup they would have received had they purchased comparable homes with a 90 percent mortgage loan at the interest rate available on the start date of their employer/employee partnership, based on the appraised value of the home on that date.

- As tenants versus owners, they would pay no down payments, carrying costs, or sales commissions before, during, or after their occupancy.

Of course, there is no way to accurately forecast where the many housing variables will be five, ten, or fifteen years in the future, but it is reasonable to expect a continuation of the volatility experienced in the past fifteen years in home prices, interest rates, and housing regulation and taxation. Employers who feel strongly that different assumptions are more realistic in their location can test out other assumptions with the idea that they shoulder the risks of residential property ownership as conservative, long-term investors with employees enjoying the benefits of living in quality, affordable housing.

This solution can be implemented on any scale by profitable companies with investment funds available. By adopting the investment dynamic discovered by the private equity investors in SFR and BFR housing while foregoing the short-term profits fueled by what-the-market-will-bear renter abuse, employers can achieve superior long-term profits by controlling payroll expenses while providing major financial and quality of life benefits for their employees. In this way companies can gain a lasting competitive advantage in almost every industry.

CHAPTER 14

WHAT ABOUT
LOW-WAGE WORKERS?

WE HAVE BEEN TALKING ABOUT RELATIVELY HIGH-wage workers. Marcus & Millichap reports that during the second half of 2022, the average monthly income of a class-A renter was about $10,000 compared to $8,100 in the first half of 2019. An important question remains: Can the solution offered here solve the housing affordability problem for low-wage workers making $15 to $22 an hour?

A worker earning $15 an hour in a full-time job makes $31,200 a year. At 30 percent of that income, affordable rent would be $780 a month, but at low-income levels, 25 percent is a more realistic affordability standard, so let's assume rent at $650 a month is needed to be affordable. A worker making $20 an hour or $41,600 a year would need $867 a month rent and at $22 an hour the rent requirement would be $953 a month.

An employer who wished to enter into a housing partnership with a worker making $15 an hour would need to be able to provide adequate housing at a cost of no more than $115,000. At $20 an hour, the housing would need to be no more than $153,000, and at $22 an hour, no more than $167,000. A short time ago, providing quality housing that meets this cost criteria was seen as impossible, but now a solution is emerging in the form of tiny home technology.

The leader in the tiny home space is a company named Boxabl, which has pioneered a new way to produce modern, easily shippable manufactured homes. Two new factories in Las Vegas, Nevada, totaling 300,000 square feet, produce their 375-square foot Casita model for around $60,000. That product can be stacked or connected to increase occupancy capacity, so including site set-up costs, homes ranging from 375 square feet to 750 square feet can be delivered furnished to be completed on site within less than a week of leaving the factory for about $85,000 to $170,000. That figure does not include land cost. Boxabl has completed an initial 156-home order for the U.S. government, and its two large assembly lines are now fully functional. This product exceeds building code requirements in all fifty states and has a large and growing waiting list based on strong customer acceptance. Other newly formed companies, like Roombus in Los Angeles, have designed attractive competing products, but are still working to start volume production. Boxabl has several different designs and different sizes in development.

The Boxabl Casita was initially designed to be an ADU unit (ADU units discussed in Chapter 9 face community impact problems, especially in older neighborhoods). Although ADU use offers the lowest land and setup cost opportunities, it does not lend itself to large-scale use as a single-family version of workforce housing. Employers who own or could purchase land suitable for residential housing or municipalities with critical affordable-housing problems would be a source of opportunities to reduce land costs. Vail's use of long-held resort land at four of its thirty-seven resorts (Park City Mountain Resort—421 units; Whistler Blackcomb—240 units; Vail Mountain—165 units; and Okemo Mountain Resort in Vermont—30 units) is a good example of locating workforce housing using owned real estate in a way that benefits the company, the employees, and the community.

The Boxabl product may have strong advantages for employers or groups of employers in smaller municipalities or rural areas.

As farms continue to increase in size and reliance on technology, they must contend with labor shortages and a broken immigration system. In the plus column, farms have land and infrastructure suited for homes like the Boxabl product. As the need for farm labor often follows changing locations as crop seasons change, moveable, affordable housing can change the economics of farming. Opportunities opened by seasonal labor situations and schools at all levels for students, teachers, and support staff also merit exploration. In addition, low-wage workers in government, manufacturing, retail, and food service, are in critical need of affordable housing.

CHAPTER 15

FINAL THOUGHTS

THE AFFORDABLE HOUSING PROBLEM IS SO LARGE and affects so many people in different ways, each individual perceives the problem differently and so judges any solution offered differently. Retirees and self-employed people may find the solution offered in this text to be inadequate since they have no employer. People whose most important concern is homelessness may reject the idea that homelessness is not an affordable housing problem but is rather a major problem that must rely on a charitable solution. Luxury homeowners may feel like their financial position excuses them from concern about a problem they don't suffer from. Since deterioration of the community support luxury housing requires has major impacts on the value of their residential investments, nothing could be farther from the truth.

The problem section of this text concentrates on real problems that have the potential for solution and discusses false problems that only detract from finding and growing a long-term solution to the affordable housing problem. Much has been written about the problems of poverty and many of those problems involve housing, but most texts emphasize a call to action to end the misery of those without the resources needed to deal with inadequate housing in today's world. It is easy to be sidetracked by compelling stories of injustice and incompetence that triumph over good intentions, but there is also a lack of actionable solutions offered. One such book is *Poverty by America* by Pulitzer Prize winning author Matthew Desmond. Professor Desmond describes the hardships of American poverty and explains why poverty persists. After identifying a long list of culprits from large corporations to lenders, he includes consumers for not boycotting the "bad guys" and doing business with only "good guys," so a lack of judgement by pretty much everyone who is not poor completes his culprit list. Specific plans like raising taxes on the wealthy to increase assistance to the poor and increasing the minimum wage seem vague and carry a long history of being hard to execute, especially in today's political world. For those seeking a deeper understanding of the problems of poverty and their effect on so many people, this is a sobering read.

Another new book entitled *America Pays a High Price for Low Wages* by Michael Lind is highly recommended to readers of *A Solution to Affordable Housing*. Mr. Lind's book does not deal directly with the affordable housing problem but sheds new light on the aspiration of workers to achieve a living wage for all. The author's discussion of how means-tested welfare programs like the earned-income tax credit (EITC), food stamps, and housing vouchers compensate for wages that are too low for workers to live on is particularly interesting and timely. These wage subsidies force taxpayers to pay to rescue workers whose work does not pay enough. The author's discussion of the "low wage/high welfare" model and the effects it has on the majority of Americans who are not poor offers valuable insights, especially for employers who have discretion in how they allocate profits among shareholders, managers and workers. For those who wish to move from studying the problem of affordable housing and related problems of poverty to solving the affordable housing problem, this is essential reading.

My text is not intended to be a forecast of the future and it does not come with a sign-up sheet for a program that will enrich the reader. Rather it is a simple idea that postulates that employers with successful businesses can produce superior long-term results by forming housing partnerships with their own employees. Unlocking the necessary financial resources by eliminating excessive lender and landlord profits which are based on the "whatever the market will bear" theory that dominates the rental and mortgage landscape today is the key. Government can join in for the benefit of government employees at all levels, including active-duty military personnel. Government may also find that the money now spent on the nation's housing problems may be better spent on homelessness as a priority and redirecting tax advantages and other policy support away from lenders, landlords and luxury homeowners to employers who chose to invest in housing solutions for their employees. The inclusion of managers is more complicated. As managerial capitalism fades and the resurgence of focused, entrepreneurial enterprise continues, employers will find less need for a high-cost manager core.

My hope is that employers will discover how rewarding it is to solve this critical problem with their employees, both in terms of financial and non-financial considerations. Employers will be further rewarded by a greatly enhanced ability to attract and retain the very best employees, who I predict can be expected to re-imagine company loyalty. I hope employees will come to understand that the real benefits of quality housing are the everyday benefits a good home provides for families while avoiding the dangers and stress of taking on excessive housing financial risk.

In his 1776 classic *The Wealth of Nations* Adam Smith said, "A man must always live by his work, and his wages must at least be sufficient to maintain him. They must even upon most occasions be somewhat more, otherwise it would be impossible for him to bring up a family, and the race of such workmen could not last beyond the first generation." Adam Smith's work remains a foundation of capitalism today and I believe it supports the solution offered in this text.

In the end, I will put my faith in Arthur Schopenhauer, and I anticipate the ridicule and opposition associated with his first two stages of reaching a true solution. I expect these initial discussions to be dominated by lenders, landlords and highly paid managers now focused on measuring and motivating workers in good times and handling worker terminations in hard times. These are the people who will see strengthening of the direct relationship between employers and workers as a direct threat to their often-excessive salaries. After that, I look forward to Schopenhauer's third stage—the solution being accepted as being self-evident.